The Spirit-Filled Follower of Jesus

DESIGN FOR DISCIPLESHIP

DFD**2**

Discipleship Inside Out®

Discipleship Inside Out®

NavPress is the publishing ministry of The Navigators, an international Christian organization and leader in personal spiritual development. NavPress is committed to helping people grow spiritually and enjoy lives of meaning and hope through personal and group resources that are biblically rooted, culturally relevant, and highly practical.

For a free catalog go to www.NavPress.com
or call 1.800.366.7788 in the United States or 1.800.839.4769 in Canada.

© 1973, 1980, 2006 by The Navigators

ISBN 978-1-60006-005-2

Cover design by Arvid Wallen
Cover illustration by Michael Halbert
Interior design by The DesignWorks Group
Creative Team: Dan Rich, Arvid Wallen, Darla Hightower, Pamela Poll, Pat Reinheimer, Kathy Guist

Original DFD Author: Chuck Broughton
Revision Team: Dennis Stokes, Judy Gomoll, Christine Weddle, Ralph Ennis

Printed in the United States of America

8 9 10 11 12 13 / 18 17 16 15 14 13

DFD2 | CONTENTS

HELPING YOU LEARN

Have you realized that you have a personal tutor at your side as you study the Bible? He is always available to help you understand what it means and how it applies to you. He is the Author of the Bible — the Holy Spirit. Jesus Christ said the Holy Spirit would "teach you all things," and "guide you into all the truth" (John 14:26; 16:13).

The Holy Spirit teaches you both in your personal study of the Bible and as you listen to God-appointed pastors and teachers. One is not a substitute for the other — you need both personal study and the teaching of others.

For your personal Bible study, you need:

- **A Time:** *Just as church attendance is planned for a regular time each week, you should also plan a time for your Bible study. Some like to study a little every day; others set aside an evening each week. Decide on a time that is best for you, then stick to it faithfully.*
- **A Place:** *If possible, choose a place free from distractions.*
- **Method:** *As you look up each verse of Scripture, think about it carefully, then write out your answer. It is also helpful to read the context (the*

surrounding verses) of each passage listed. Write the answers in your own words whenever possible.

- **Material:** *Beside your study book, you will need a complete Bible—Old and New Testaments.*

In Book One, *Your Life in Christ,* you discovered the reasons for the central place Christ holds in your life. But you may have wondered how to live a Spirit-filled, Christ-centered life. In this study you will find answers to this question in five important areas:

- *The Obedient Follower of Jesus*
- *God's Word in Your Life*
- *Conversing with God*
- *Fellowship with Followers of Jesus*
- *Witnessing*

Ask for the Spirit's guidance as you study. Psalm 119:18 is a good prayer: "Open my eyes that I may see wonderful things in your law."

As we discovered in Book One, having Jesus at the very core of our lives empowers us to live the Spirit-filled life. Just as the driving force of a wheel comes from the hub, so our source of power comes from Christ.

The spokes radiating from **CHRIST** are some means through which we experience God's grace and transformation. As we keep Him central, beholding and worshiping Him 24/7, our intimacy with God deepens. The vertical spokes are key to enjoying our relationship with God.

The **WORD** helps us to know God and to experience His truth. It nourishes us spiritually and equips us for spiritual battle. God is present in His living Word as a dynamic force to transform and protect our lives. The Holy Spirit guides us and engages our hearts as we connect with God's Word.

Through **PRAYER** we talk to our heavenly Father, offering Him our praise, thanks, and needs. God listens and responds by speaking

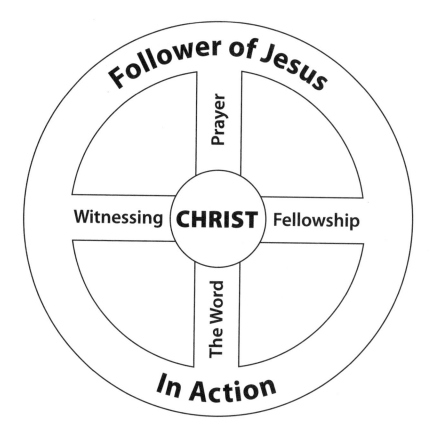

comfort, truth, and hope into our hearts. This process also deepens our intimacy with God and builds our trust. When we don't know what to pray, the Holy Spirit intercedes for us.

The horizontal spokes are about our relationships with those who follow Jesus and those who do not yet know Him.

True **FELLOWSHIP** allows love and humility to flow in ways that protect our hearts. Through this community we can both give and receive encouragement, guidance, and truth. God uses these relationships to meet needs, help us grow, and to captivate the interest of a watching world.

As God meets us with His good news, we are transformed toward Christlikeness. From the overflow of this relationship, we can partner with

God by spreading the gospel of Jesus and His Kingdom. In **WITNESS-ING** we share with others our own experience and the wonderful truths of God.

These all converge in the rim of the wheel. Our living daily **OBEDIENCE** connects with the road of life to bring glory to God.

The Obedient Follower of Jesus

At the moment you placed your faith in Jesus Christ as your Savior, a life of authentic obedience to God became a real possibility. The Holy Spirit set you free from the bondage of sin, shame, and death (Romans 8:2). He enables you to live a Christlike life.

> It is not just that we should strive to live like Jesus, but that Jesus by his Spirit should come and live in us. To have him as our example is not enough; we need him as our Savior. It is thus through his atoning death that the penalty of our sins may be forgiven; whereas it is through his indwelling Spirit that the power of our sins may be broken.
>
> — John R. W. Stott*

---

* John R. W. Stott, *Basic Christianity* (London: InterVarsity Christian Fellowship, 1958), 105.

As you learn more about the obedient believer in action, remember that the Holy Spirit will help you obey.

A BASIS FOR OBEDIENCE: BEHOLDING GOD

The sincere desire to obey God begins by remembering who He is and what He desires for you.

1. What do the following passages tell you about God?

a. Romans 11:33-36

b. Revelation 1:17-18

c. Revelation 4:11

d. How do these glimpses of God's character influence your obedience to Him?

2. Read Deuteronomy 26:16-19.

a. How is the relationship between God and His people described?

b. What did God expect of His people (behavior and attitudes)?

c. What did God promise His people?

3. Read Psalm 40:7-8 to discover how David responded to God's call for obedience. Now write in your own words how your heart responds to God's call for obedience.

4. Reflect on John 14:15 and 14:21. Try to express the relationship between loving God and obeying Him.

5. God not only loves us — He loves us jealously! For our own good He doesn't want anything or anyone to steal His place in our hearts and devotion. In light of the verses below, what is positive about God being the jealous Lover of your soul?

"Do not worship any other god, for the LORD, whose name is Jealous, is a jealous God." (Exodus 34:14)

You're cheating on God. If all you want is your own way, flirting with the world every chance you get, you end up enemies of God and his way. And do you suppose God doesn't care? The proverb has it that "he's a fiercely jealous lover." And what he gives in love is far better than anything else you'll find. (James 4:4-5, MSG)

How would your story be different if God were not jealous for you?

6. As you look back on your spiritual journey so far, what has your disobedience to God cost you? How have your choices of obedience benefited you?

 Compliance sounds like 'OK, OK. I'll do it. But it won't be pretty. I'll do it, but this story is not over. Someone, sometime, somewhere, is gonna pay . . .' Obedience from the heart says, 'I'll do this because I trust you and believe it is for our best.'

—Bill Thrall, Ken McElrath, Bruce McNicol,
Beyond Your Best

7. Which do you think God prefers from you: reluctant compliance or trusting obedience? Why?

OBEYING GOD'S DESIRES FOR YOUR LIFE

How do you know God's desires for your life? The Bible is God's revelation of truth, and obedience to God's Word is obedience to God Himself.

8. Psalm 119 deals with the importance of God's Word. What are several ways the Bible can help you live well for Christ?

Verse 11

Verse 105

Verse 130

9. In 2 Timothy 3:16 Paul said that the Scriptures are profitable for:

a. _____ (what to believe and do)

b._____ (exposing sin)

c._____ (how to change)

d._____ (how to live)

This can be illustrated in the following manner:

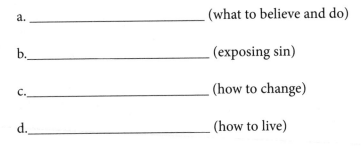

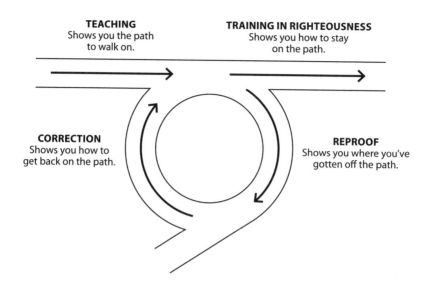

TEACHING
Shows you the path
to walk on.

TRAINING IN RIGHTEOUSNESS
Shows you how to stay
on the path.

CORRECTION
Shows you how to
get back on the path.

REPROOF
Shows you where you've
gotten off the path.

10. Perhaps God's Word has made you aware of an area of your life that needs to be brought into closer obedience to God. If so, in what area?

11. What do you see in these verses about God's will and commands for you that motivate you to trust and obey Him?

Jeremiah 29:11

Romans 12:2

1 John 5:3

Is there anything about God's will and commands for you that is frightening? Explain.

What makes God's will and commands good for you?

12. God does not expect you to live an obedient life in your own strength. He has provided you with everything necessary to make obedience a reality. In addition to His personal presence, what else has God given to help you live for Him? Match the letter with the appropriate reference.

____ 2 Timothy 1:7

a. Everything we need for a godly life

____ 2 Peter 1:3

b. The Scriptures

____ Romans 15:4

c. Power, love, and self-discipline

____ 1 John 4:4

d. Power to overcome our worldly enemy

____ 2 Corinthians 6:16

e. God living in us

LIVING OBEDIENTLY

The obedient follower of Jesus still faces daily struggles with temptation. With God's help, we can practice obedience and gain victory over sin.

13. Discover the source and causes of temptation in the following verses:

a. Who is the tempter? (Matthew 4:1-3)

b. Who is never the source of temptation? (James 1:13)

c. What causes you to be drawn into temptation? (James 1:14)

14. In Joshua 7:20-21, examine Achan's statement about his disobedience.

a. What factors contributed to his disobedience?

b. At what point could he have prevented his sin?

c. What can you learn from his error?

15. Using the following verses as a guide, write a brief definition of sin. (Isaiah 53:6; James 4:17; and 1 John 3:4)

How does sin differ from temptation?

16. Consider 1 Corinthians 10:13.

    a. Are the temptations you face different or more difficult than what others face?

b. What limit does God place on temptation?

c. What is God sure to provide when you are tempted?

17. In 1 John 1:9 we are told to . . . (Check the correct answer.)

____ feel badly about sin.

____ try to do something to make up for sin.

____ confess sin to God.

____ try to forget about sin.

Why is this important?

18. In Psalm 32:5, David prays and confesses his sin. Write this verse in your own words.

The practice of walking in victory can be pictured as follows.

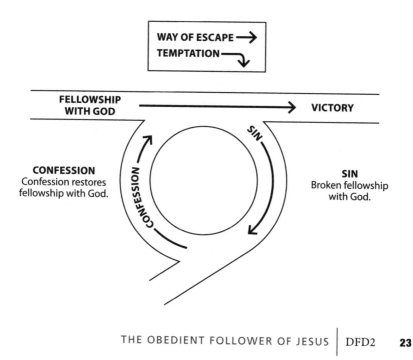

19. In what practical ways can you avoid falling into temptation and begin walking in victory?

Proverbs 4:13-15

James 4:7

TO SUBMIT TO GOD you must yield your will to God's will.
TO RESIST THE DEVIL you must use God's provision for victory.

20. These questions about sin and temptation probably remind you of the daily conflict you experience.

a. Review question 10. What is the root problem in the area you recorded?

b. How does the temptation to disobey God in this area begin to show itself?

c. What steps can you take to avoid these beginnings?

Walk by the Spirit, and you will not gratify the desires of the flesh. (Galatians 5:16)

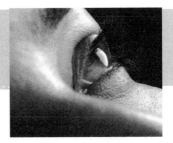
1 John 1:9

If we confess our sins, he is faithful and just and will forgive
us our sins and purify us from all unrighteousness.

1 John 1:9

Making a commitment to a person is basic to any long-term relationship. It is no different with God, who is your Creator, your Lord, and the Lover of your soul. He has made an eternal commitment to His people and has sealed it through the work of Christ and the indwelling Holy Spirit. He desires for us to commit ourselves to following Jesus and the ways of Jesus. As you reflect on your journey with God, journal about where you are right now in your commitment to follow Him, to obey His ways, and to love this Lover of your soul.

► Your obedience to God is based on the fact that He is your Creator, Lord, and the Lover of your soul. You obey Him because of who He is. He is simply worthy of our obedience.

► God reveals His ways through the Scriptures, and His commands are good.

► To the extent that you appropriate God's good provision for victory, you can experience a life of trusting and obeying Him.

► You are not immune, however, to temptation and sin. Sin does not negate God's love for you, but it does break your fellowship with Him. Confession restores that fellowship.

Jesus presents a vivid picture of two types of people in Matthew 7:24-27: the wise man and the foolish man. Read the passage and answer the following questions.

	Wise Man	Foolish Man
What foundation did he build his house on?		
What do you think each foundation represents?		
What forces was his house exposed to?		
What happened to his house?		
Did this person hear God's Word?		
How did he respond to God's Word?		

What do you sense God saying to you through this story based on how you are building your life?

2

God's Word in Your Life

Moses expressed how crucial and significant God's Word was to the people he led in Deuteronomy 32:47: "They are not just idle words for you — they are your *life*. By them you will live long in the land you are crossing the Jordan to possess" (emphasis added).

Soldiers in battle used their swords as both an offensive and a defensive weapon. God has equipped you with such a weapon for your spiritual battle: "the sword of the Spirit, which is the word of God" (Ephesians 6:17). The Holy Spirit uses the Word of God to accomplish the work of God.

> The great need of the hour among persons spiritually hungry is twofold: first, to know the Scriptures, apart from which no saving truth will be vouchsafed by our Lord; the second, to be enlightened by the Spirit, apart from whom the Scriptures will not be understood.
>
> — A. W. Tozer[*]

[*] A. W. Tozer, *The Root of the Righteous* (Harrisburg, PA: Christian Publications, 1955), 37.

GOD'S WORD — HIS COMMUNICATION TO YOU

The Bible is the most remarkable book ever written. In fact, it is a whole library consisting of sixty-six books! The writing was done by about forty people from many occupations and all walks of life — farmers and fishermen, teachers and physicians, public officials and kings. They wrote over a period of approximately 1,500 years and in three languages — Hebrew, Aramaic, and Greek. They wrote on many subjects (including religion, history, law, and science) and in many genre (including biography, prophecy, poetry, and drama). With all this diversity, it is amazing that the Bible is "as harmoniously united as the parts that make up a human body." That is because the Bible has one great theme and central figure — Jesus Christ. All of this would be impossible unless the Bible had one supreme Author — and it did: the Holy Spirit of God.

1. What does 2 Timothy 3:16 say about the Scriptures? (Circle the letter of the correct answer.)

   a. Some of the Bible is inspired by God.

   b. All of it is inspired by God.

   c. Only the parts that speak to you in a personal way are inspired by God.

According to this verse, what are the Scriptures useful for in our lives?

> **Inspired** comes from a Greek word meaning "God-breathed." The meaning, then, is not that God breathed into the writers, nor that he somehow breathed into the writings to give them their special character, but that what was written by men was breathed out by God. He spoke through them. They were his spokesmen.
>
> —John R. W. Stott,
> *Understanding the Bible*

2. How was Scripture given? (2 Peter 1:20-21)

Who, then, helps you understand the Bible?
(1 Corinthians 2:12-13)

THE BIBLE AT A GLANCE (66 BOOKS)

"The New is in the Old concealed.
The Old is in the New revealed."

Old Testament (39 books)

HISTORY 17 books	POETRY 5 books	PROPHECY 17 books
Law	Job	**Major Prophets**
Genesis	Psalms	Isaiah
Exodus	Proverbs	Jeremiah
Leviticus	Ecclesiastes	Lamentations
Numbers	Song of	Ezekiel
Deuteronomy	Solomon	Daniel
History and Government		**Minor Prophets**
Joshua		Hosea
Judges		Joel
Ruth		Amos
I Samuel		Obadiah
2 Samuel		Jonah
I Kings		Micah
2 Kings		Nahum
I Chronicles		Habakkuk
2 Chronicles		Zephaniah
Ezra		Haggai
Nehemiah		Zechariah
Esther		Malachi

The Old Testament looks forward to
Christ's sacrifice on the cross.

The New Testament is based on
the work Christ finished on the cross.

About 400 years
between testaments

New Testament (27 books)

HISTORY 5 books	TEACHING 21 books	PROPHECY 1 book
Gospels	**Paul's Letters**	Revelation
Matthew	Romans	
Mark	I Corinthians	
Luke	2 Corinthians	
John	Galatians	
	Ephesians	
The Early Church	Philippians	
Acts	Colossians	
	I Thessalonians	
	2 Thessalonians	
	I Timothy	
	2 Timothy	
	Titus	
	Philemon	
	General Letters	
	Hebrews	
	James	
	I Peter	
	2 Peter	
	1, 2, 3 John	
	Jude	

God used forty different men over a period of 1,500 years (about 1400 B.C. to A.D. 90) in writing the Bible.

From *Understanding the Bible* (London: Scripture Union, 1972), 183.

3. How do the following verses describe God's Word?

Matthew 24:35

John 17:17

4. What do you think it means that the Word of God is "alive"? (Hebrews 4:12)

5. Examine Psalm 19:7-11 carefully. Use the following chart to aid you in your investigation.

Verse	What the Bible Is Called	Its Characteristics	What It Will Do for Me
7	law	perfect	refreshed spiritually
	statutes	trustworthy	gives wisdom
8			
9			
10			
11			

In the chart above place a check by the two or three thoughts that impressed you most about the Bible. Then journal about why this impressed you.

6. The Bible is like a love letter from God. In it He reveals Himself, His purposes, and His plans. As you read any passage of Scripture, consider this question: What does this passage have to say about who God is and what is on His heart? Try this as you read 1 Peter 1:3-5.

> " When we begin to recognize the bridal theme that is woven throughout the Bible, it will not only change the way we read Scripture, but it will also enable us to understand and experience the romance of redemption.
>
> —S. J. Hill, *Burning Desire*

7. Look up the following verses and summarize some of the ways the Bible is important to you as a follower of Jesus.

John 5:39

2 Peter 1:4

1 John 2:1

8. A metaphor explains something by comparing one thing with something similar and usually tangible. In the following verses, what is God's Word compared with? What is the function of these objects?

Verse	Object	Function
Jeremiah 23:29		
Matthew 4:4		
James 1:23-25		
Hebrews 4:12		

Which of these metaphors for the Bible connects with your experience? Explain.

BECOMING A MAN OR WOMAN OF THE WORD

9. If you could turn to just one place in Scripture that describes the living Word of God, Psalm 119 would be a great place to start. Nearly every verse in this psalm speaks of His Word and about applying it in daily living. Notice the psalmist's attitudes and actions concerning God's Word. Beginning with verse 11, fill in the diagram below.

Verse	Attitude	Action
9	Keeping God's Word	Pure life
10	Wholeheartedly sought God	Prayed— "Don't let me wander"
11		
12		
13		
14		
15		
16		

10. According to John 8:31-32, what characterizes a follower of Jesus?

How would you explain these words to another person?

11. From the following verses, fill in the remaining blanks.

Verse	Action to Take	Why
Psalm 78:5-7		
Acts 17:11		
James 1:22		
Revelation 1:3		

12. Ezra is a good example of a man who felt a responsibility toward God's Word. What was his approach to Scripture? (Ezra 7:10)

Note the order of Ezra's actions. He applied the Scriptures to his own life before he taught them to others. Why do you think that is important?

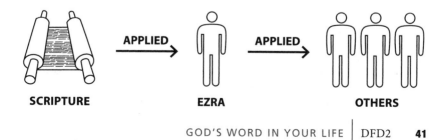

SCRIPTURE   APPLIED   EZRA   APPLIED   OTHERS

13. Reflect carefully on Colossians 3:16. What practical steps can you take to allow Christ's Word to dwell in you richly? (Examples: take notes during sermons, write out memory verses)

During the next week, how can you put one of these methods into practice?

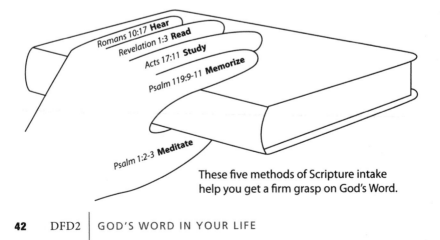

These five methods of Scripture intake help you get a firm grasp on God's Word.

THE IMPORTANCE OF MEDITATION

Meditation on the Scriptures is prayerful reflection with a view to understanding and application. The primary purpose is to know God deeply and to live your life within God's will by prayerfully thinking on how to relate God's Word to yourself.

14. From Joshua 1:8, answer the following questions.

   a. What should you meditate on?

   b. Explain the relationship between meditation and application.

c. What are the results of meditation?

15. Learning to ask your own questions will deepen your meditation on God's Word. Meditate on Psalm 1, and record your findings. Here are some questions to help you get started:

How is the follower of Jesus to be like a tree?

What are the differences between the godly and the ungodly person as to habits, stability, and future?

What new ideas from this psalm will help you in your relationship with God?

Another question of your own:

In the space below, draw a simple picture that depicts the content of verses 2 and 3.

16. Notice the response of Jeremiah's heart in Jeremiah 15:16. How do you think your heart can respond to the words of God?

Psalm 119:9-11

How can a young person stay on the path of purity? By living according to your word. I seek you with all my heart; do not let me stray from your commands. I have hidden your word in my heart that I might not sin against you.

Psalm 119:9-11

Read Psalm 19:1-6 and ponder how God reveals Himself to us through nature. Then read Psalm 19:7-11 and consider how He reveals Himself to us through Scripture. In listening to God's silent language in nature, it is helpful to ask, "What does this aspect of nature have to silently say about who God is and who I am?" For example consider the flowers of the field, and meditate on Isaiah 40:6-8. What do flowers have to silently say about who God is and who I am? Repeat for other ordinary aspects of life, such as sleep, clothes, food, and so on.

POINTS TO REMEMBER

▸ God has communicated to people through His Word — the Bible.

▸ The Bible is a love letter from God the Father to His children. It is to be read as a personal communication from Him.

▸ Through the Scriptures you can get to know God better, understand His desires for your life, and discover new truths about living for Him.

▸ God commands believers to let His Word dwell richly in them. So it is important to give yourself wholeheartedly to allowing God's Word to fill your life.

▸ God places emphasis on the act of meditating in His Word, because effective meditation leads to personal application.

Reading systematically through the Bible (yes, the *whole* Bible!) can give you an overall view of God's message. If you've never read through the Bible, you might want to start with the New Testament first. This will give you a context for reading and understanding the Old Testament. You might want to try an easy-to-read Bible translation such as *The New International Version* (NIV), *The New Living Translation* (NLT), or *The Message* (MSG). Choose a reading pace that is realistic. Use a simple chart to keep track of which books and chapters you read.

Here's a challenge. If you read the Bible for only fifteen to twenty minutes a day (about what we spend reading the newspaper or checking e-mail), you can finish the New Testament in about three months.

Here's a bigger challenge. Why not set yourself a goal to read through the whole Bible every year for the next three years? Only fifteen minutes a day will get you there!

CHAPTER

3

Conversing with God

Communication is essential for any growing relationship, including our relationship with God. Prayer is our means of speaking to God and listening as He speaks to us.

> The Spirit links himself with us in our praying and pours his supplications into our own. We may master the technique of prayer and understand its philosophy; we may have unlimited confidence in the veracity and validity of the promises concerning prayer. We may plead them earnestly. But if we ignore the part played by the Holy Spirit, we have failed to use the master key.
>
> — J. Oswald Sanders*

---

* J. Oswald Sanders, *Spiritual Leadership* (Chicago: Moody, 1967), 79.

PRAYER — YOUR TWO-WAY COMMUNICATION WITH GOD

1. As a believer in Christ you have been given a special opportunity, according to Hebrews 4:15-16. From this passage, what are several things that encourage you about coming to God in prayer?

2. Because God is the believer's refuge, what are you told to do? (Psalm 18:2-3)

Do you feel you need a refuge? Why or why not?

3. God is present everywhere (see Psalm 139:7-10). How might this reality impact your practice of praying?

How does 1 Thessalonians 5:17 relate to this reality?

 The best prayers often have more groans than words.

—John Bunyan

4. What are some emotions you can discuss with God?

5. When you pray, the Holy Spirit helps you know what to say and how to say it (Romans 8:26-27). How does this encourage you?

6. What attitudes can you have in coming to God?

Psalm 27:8

Psalm 46:10

Psalm 63:1

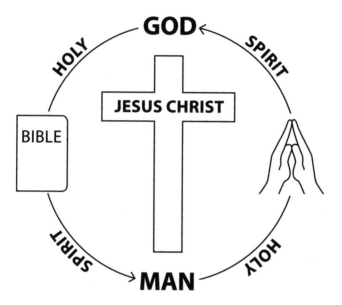

What truths are illustrated by this diagram?

THE BENEFITS
OF PRAYER

We believers have the privilege of talking with God about everything. We also experience great benefits from our communion with God.

7. If you could spend an hour with God and say anything at all, what would you say? What would you ask Him?

8. Different types of prayer are necessary to communicate the variety of thoughts and feelings you want to express. Match each reference with the corresponding type of prayer.

Praise (for who God is)	Psalm 38:18
Thanksgiving (for what He has done)	Hebrews 13:15
Confession	James 1:5
Prayer for others	Ephesians 5:20
Prayer for personal needs	1 Samuel 12:23

9. What truth do you find both in Jeremiah 33:3 and Ephesians 3:20?

10. What results did the psalmist experience when he prayed? (Psalm 34:4-7)

11. Paul wrote in Philippians 4:6-7 about a powerful key to freedom from anxiety.

   a. What are you to do?

b. Why do you feel God is interested in every area of your life?

c. What is God's promise and how can this protect you?

d. In what area can you immediately begin to apply this truth?

12. What conditions of prayer do you find in the following verses?

Psalm 66:18

Matthew 21:22

John 15:7

John 16:24

James 5:16

1 John 5:14-15

13. Even when conditions are met, it sometimes appears as if God is not answering prayer. But remember that "no" and "wait" are as much of an answer as "yes." Has God ever answered "no" to your request and later you realized "no" was a good answer? Explain.

" Faithful servants have a way of knowing answered prayer when they see it, and a way of not giving up when they don't.

—Max Lucado

14. Consider Jesus' pattern for prayer in Matthew 6:9-13.

   a. How does the prayer begin? Why is this important?

   b. Which requests are God-centered?

   c. Which requests are people-centered?

   d. How can this pattern for praying help you pray?

> Prayer means yearning for the simple presence of God, for a personal understanding of His Word, for knowledge of His will and for capacity to hear and obey Him.
>
> —Thomas Merton

FOR WHOM DO YOU PRAY?

15. What did Paul desire for those who didn't know Christ? (Romans 10:1)

What did he do about it?

16. Read 1 Timothy 2:1-4. What groups of people should you pray for? Why?

17. What does the Lord desire you to pray for? (Matthew 9:37-38)

Why do you think this is important?

18. Read Luke 6:28. Are there people in your life who have mistreated you? Spend some time now talking with God about them and your response to them.

19. Using Paul's prayer in Ephesians 3:14-21 as a guideline, list some requests you could pray for others and for yourself.

20. Have you tried using a prayer list along with a column to track God's answer? A list can help you remember things you might otherwise forget to pray about. It can include:

- *Your family*
- *Your nonbelieving friends and acquaintances*
- *Your pastor and church and group you study with*
- *Believers you know*
- *Those who oppose you*
- *Governmental authorities*
- *Your personal needs*

21. From what you have already learned in *Design for Discipleship*, record several reasons why you need to spend daily time with God — meditating on His Word and conversing with Him in prayer.

Hebrews 4:16

Let us then approach God's throne of grace with confidence, so that we may receive mercy and find grace to help us in our time of need.

Hebrews 4:16

Talking to God is only part of prayer. The other part is learning to be still in His presence so that you can hear what He is saying to your heart. The verses below will help to quiet your heart. Take some time now to pray. Linger in the presence of God. Listen and pray. Later record some of your experience with Him.

"Be still, and know that I am God." (Psalm 46:10)

My heart is not proud, LORD, my eyes are not haughty; I do not concern myself with great matters or things too wonderful for me. But I have calmed and quieted myself, I am like a weaned child with its mother; like a weaned child I am content. (Psalm 131:1-2)

► God desires your fellowship. So He has provided prayer as the means of communicating directly with Him and growing in intimacy with Him.

► Prayer releases us from fear and worry.

► The Scriptures provide numerous patterns and examples for our prayer.

► Regular times alone with God — both pouring out your heart and listening to Him speak into your heart — are vitally necessary for your spiritual growth.

Sometimes we hesitate to pour out our hearts to God for fear that some of our thoughts or feelings are not appropriate to express. But the writers of the Psalms didn't hesitate to be authentic with God emotionally. The Psalms contain many passionate prayers. Some start with songs and praise. Some are quite raw with concerns and pleas at the beginning of the Psalm, but then they circle back reflectively at the end. Questions and confidence are seen together as the writer processes issues and struggles before God.

For instance, check out Psalm 10, 13, 69, or 142. How does this help you to have freedom before God in prayer?

> The ranting and raving, the passion and ecstasy, the fury and desolation found in the Psalms are so far from our religious expression that it seems hard to believe they were given to us as our *guide* to prayer. They seem so, well, *desperate*.
>
> —John Eldredge,
> *The Journey of Desire*

Fellowship with Followers of Jesus

In light of all this, here's what I want you to do. While I'm locked up here, a prisoner for the Master, I want you to get out there and walk—better yet, run!—on the road God called you to travel. I don't want any of you sitting around on your hands. I don't want anyone strolling off, down some path that goes nowhere. And mark that you do this with humility and discipline—not in fits and starts, but steadily, pouring yourselves out for each other in acts of love, alert at noticing differences and quick at mending fences. You were all called to travel on the same road and in the same direction, so stay together, both outwardly and inwardly. You have one Master, one faith, one baptism, one God and Father of all, who rules over all, works through all, and is present in all. Everything you are and think and do is permeated with Oneness. But that doesn't mean you should all look and speak and act the same. Out of the generosity of Christ, each of us is given his own gift. (Ephesians 4:1-7, MSG)

WHAT IS BIBLICAL FELLOWSHIP?

1. In the passage on the previous page, what does the apostle Paul urge us to do as part of God's family?

   What does he warn us not to be doing?

   What binds us together in oneness?

2. Read Romans 12:10-13. If you were involved in a community like this, how would it be beneficial to you? To others?

3. *Fellowship* is derived from the Greek word *koinonia*, which means "sharing in common." God has given you much to share. As you examine the verses below, determine what you can share with others and one practical way to share it.

Verse	What to Share	A Way to Share
1 John 4:11, 21		
Galatians 6:2		
Galatians 6:6		
James 5:16		

4. Recall an incident when you resisted someone who genuinely wanted to help you out. Did your attitude hinder his or her attempt at sharing? If so, how?

Sharing involves giving and receiving, and both are integral parts of meaningful fellowship. Which is easier for you — to give or receive? Explain.

> **❝❝** Love makes your soul crawl from its hiding place.
>
> —Zora Neale Hurston

5. Believers fellowship together on the basis that they are all forgiven sinners — forgiven, yes, but still sinners. Followers of Jesus can honestly share their lives lovingly. You don't have to pretend to be something you are not. Knowing this fact, what is your responsibility toward your brother or sister when you have offended him or her? (Matthew 5:22-24)

(In the *King James*, *Raca* is a term expressing contempt for someone.)

What is your responsibility when he has offended you? (Matthew 18:15,35)

6. Picture the following situation. Several followers of Jesus are in the same room drinking coffee and eating doughnuts as they discuss last week's championship game. The conversation moves to the subject of "which animal makes the best household pet." Then one of them tells a joke he recently heard. They enjoy a good laugh together and begin to talk about the weather forecast for tomorrow. As one of them leaves, he says, "It sure is good to have fellowship!"

a. Is this genuine biblical fellowship?

b. Why or why not?

c. Could this fellowship be improved? How?

7. Why is fellowship with others in God's family so important?

Proverbs 27:17

Ecclesiastes 4:9-10

8. What is the purpose of meeting together as believers? (Hebrews 10:24-25)

9. In studying a verse, it is often helpful to locate other verses elsewhere in the Bible that relate directly to the one being examined. The other verses are called cross-references. Hebrews 3:13 is a cross-reference to Hebrews 10:24-25. From this cross-reference, why is it necessary to encourage one another daily?

10. Explain why fellowship is important to you. How have you benefited from relating to other followers of Jesus?

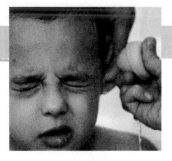

11. God uses the analogy of a body to describe the relationship of believers with one another and with Christ. Who is the head of the body? What does this mean? (Colossians 1:18-19)

Think of what happens when you hit your finger with a hammer. How does this affect the entire body?

12. Each believer is given different but important opportunities and responsibilities in this spiritual body, the church. Read 1 Corinthians 12:14-27.

a. Who gave the members their various functions? (verse 18)

b. What are some of His desires? (verse 24-26)

c. What attitudes can lead to disharmony in the body? (verses 15,16,21)

d. Do you ever struggle with feeling superior or inferior to others in the body of Christ whose functions are different from yours? If so, how do you deal with these feelings? (verses 20-22)

13. The body works together as one unit, yet it has many specialized organs that perform diverse functions. Summarize in a few sentences how this God-given combination of unity and diversity can provide both safety and interdependence.

14. According to Ephesians 4:2-3, what will preserve unity in the body?

How do you practice being "completely humble" as a follower of Jesus?

15. Examine your attitudes toward other believers. Is there someone you find difficult to relate to in love as another member of Christ's body? Why?

What steps can you take to bring harmony to your relationship with this individual?

How good and pleasant it is when God's people live together in unity! (Psalm 133:1)

16. What activities of the church in Jerusalem are mentioned in Acts 2:42-47?

From these activities, what would you describe as several distinguishing marks of the early church?

1. Generosity

2. Love

3.

4.

5.

17. Read Ephesians 4:11-16.

    a. Who is to equip the saints so they can do the work of the ministry? (verse 11)

    b. What are some of the ultimate goals of biblical community? (verse 13-16)

    c. What particular "work of service" (verse 12) are you active in right now that God is using to build up others in the body of Christ?

18. Examine 1 Peter 5:1-9. This passage gives direction to the leaders and members of a "flock." Using the following chart, contrast the right and wrong ways of demonstrating leadership.

Verse	Right Way	Wrong Way

What is your responsibility to your spiritual elders? (verse 5)

19. Meditate on 1 Corinthians 9:11,14 about the support of those who are appointed to preach and teach in the family of God.

a. What instructions are you given?

b. Are you presently giving back to God part of what He is giving you?

c. What does God want you to do with regard to prayer and financial support for your spiritual leaders?

20. In Colossians 4:3-4, Paul requested prayer for his ministry.

a. Paraphrase his request.

b. Stop a moment. Use this request as a basis to pray for another believer. Record the person's name here.

c. What is one thing you can do during this week to encourage those who are helping you walk with Christ?

> **❝❞** Each Christian should select his church because he is convinced that within its particular structure he will find the greatest opportunities for spiritual growth, the greatest satisfactions for his human needs, and the greatest chance to be of helpful service to those around him.
>
> —Billy Graham, *Peace with God*

Hebrews 10:24-25

And let us consider how we may spur one another on toward love and good deeds, not giving up meeting together, as some are in the habit of doing, but encouraging one another—and all the more as you see the Day approaching.

Hebrews 10:24-25

MY JOURNAL

Pause for a while to think about two or three people whom God has used to build you up in your walk with Christ. Imagine where you would be right now without their influence. Prayerfully and thankfully journal about this provision of grace through your fellowship with each of them. Also journal about how you are influencing others for God right now — or would like to.

▶ Genuine fellowship or biblical community is based on the concept of giving to and receiving from other followers of Jesus. You can share with others whatever God has given you — forgiveness, mercy, possessions, love, His Word, and many other things.

▶ God gives fellowship for the purpose of mutual encouragement and growth.

▶ He wants believers to live in unity and harmony with one another. To help us understand how believers are related, God uses the analogy of the body. Jesus Christ is the Head of the body, which is comprised of all believers. This provides both safety and interdependence.

▶ All followers of Jesus throughout the world belong to Christ's body, but it is important for you to recognize how God wants you to be related to a smaller, specific group of believers. This smaller group is for the purpose of instruction, sharing, worship, and service. God has given spiritual leaders to help you mature in Christ and to become effective in the ministry.

In Paul's day one of the issues concerning fellowship among believers was the cultural divide between Jews and Greeks. In our world there are often cultural and racial issues that hinder believers from sharing their lives with one another. What cultural or racial divides have you experienced? How can you work to overcome these divides for greater love?

5

Witnessing

Have you ever thought of witnessing not in terms of salesmanship or persuasion, but as . . . matchmaking? At its very heart, witnessing is the process and privilege of introducing the Bridegroom (Jesus) to prospective brides (nonbelievers). After all, Jesus truly is the Lover of souls, wooing His chosen beloved into permanent surrender with His self-sacrifice and unfailing love. If we ignore the wooing and try to force a union, we may miss this very heart of the new life in and with Jesus Christ.*

---

* Adapted from Judy Gomoll, "Matchmaker! Matchmaker!" *Discipleship Journal*, issue 57, 28.

1. In Mark 5:18-19, notice Jesus' words to a man he had healed. Why do you think Jesus gave these directives? (Also 1 John 1:3)

How would you express what the Lord has done for you and how He has had mercy on you recently?

> Witnessing is taking a good look at the Lord Jesus and then telling others what you've seen.

2. Carefully examine 2 Corinthians 5:9-14. In this section Paul lists several motivations and reasons for witnessing. List those you discover.

Verse 9

Verse 10

Verse 11

Verse 14

3. Two ways of witnessing are described in the New Testament. The apostles went (usually as teams) across cultural barriers into places and to people who had never heard of Christ. Typically they came to a major city as outsiders, proclaimed the gospel boldly, established a foundation generation of believers there, and then moved on. Read Colossians 4:3-4 as one example of "mobile" evangelism. What did Paul ask the believers at Colosse to pray for him and his team of evangelists?

4. The other way to witness described in the New Testament usually occurred after these apostolic teams "left town." They entrusted the local believers to carry the gospel into their unique family, social, and work networks along relational lines. Read Colossians 4:2,5-6. What practical advice does Paul give the local believers regarding advancing the gospel right where they lived?

5. Where and how do you see both approaches to witnessing being appropriate today?

Mobile / apostolic approach:

Local / insider approach:

> The great mission of Christianity was in reality accomplished by means of informal missionaries chattering to friends and chance acquaintances in homes, and in wine shops, on walks, and around market stalls. They went everywhere gossiping the gospel; and they did it naturally . . . and with the conviction of those who are not paid to say that sort of thing.
>
> —Michael Green,
> *Evangelism in the Early Church*

6. As you read the quote on the previous page regarding the early church, think about God's loving purposes. How would you like to participate?

7. One's attitude can make all the difference in witnessing. In each example below, describe how people acted and why they acted this way.

The authorities (John 12:42-43)

Paul (Romans 1:15-16)

What was the primary difference in attitude between Paul and the authorities?

HOW DO YOU EFFECTIVELY WITNESS?

Witnessing is not merely an activity — it is a way of life. Followers of Jesus don't *do* witnessing; they *are* witnesses — good or bad.

We will not be effective "going to" lost people until we are effective in sharing our faith naturally right where we are, among those who know us best. Some people never read the Bible and don't attend church. If you want them to know what Christ can do for them, let them see what Christ has done for you.

WITNESSING THROUGH LOVE

8. Consider the qualities of love mentioned in 1 Corinthians 13:4-7. Which three do you think characterize you most often as you try to be an effective witness?

9. Read John 13:34-35. Imagine yourself as one of the apostles, and Jesus has just finished making this statement. What immediately comes to your mind?

Why do you think Jesus gave this command?

 Preach the gospel at all times. If necessary, use words.

—Attributed to Saint Francis of Assisi

10. What can be the results of your good works? (Matthew 5:16)

11. As a follower of Jesus, you are witnessing to others by the way you live life. What do you think nonbelievers perceive about Jesus from your lifestyle alone?

12. What ambition did Paul desire for those at Thessalonica and why? (1 Thessalonians 4:11-12)

What are your ambitions and why?

> You are writing a gospel, a chapter each day,
> by the deeds that you do and the words that you say.
> Men read what you write—distorted or true;
> What is the gospel according to you?

—Anonymous

WITNESSING BY WORD

13. When you think about witnessing to others, how do you react?
    (Either check a given sentence or write one of your own.)

    ___ I find it difficult to speak of such a personal matter.

    ___ I do not speak unless someone asks me.

    ___ I find it easy to talk to friends about Christ, but not people I
    don't know.

    ___ I find it easy to talk to strangers about Christ, but not close
    friends.

    ___ I often find myself talking to people about Christ, and I enjoy
    it very much.

How do you think Peter would have answered this question?
(Acts 4:20)

What most hinders you from witnessing verbally with others?

14. What challenge and instruction do you see in 1 Peter 3:15?

15. Paul gave some important foundations about witnessing in 1 Corinthians 2:4-5. Write these verses in your own words.

16. The blind man whom Jesus healed had little or no theological training, but he was able to express simply and effectively the facts of his experience. What did he say? (John 9:25)

Even without extensive theological training, how can you express your experience with Christ to others?

> I cannot, by being good, tell men of Jesus' atoning death and resurrection, nor of my faith in his divinity. The emphasis is too much on me, and too little on him.
>
> —Samuel Shoemaker,
> *Extraordinary Living for Ordinary Men*

PAUL'S STORY

17. According to 1 Corinthians 15:1-4, what is the essence of the gospel?

18. Read the account of Paul standing before King Agrippa and his royal party in Acts 26:1-29, then answer the following questions.

    a. How did Paul begin his story? (verses 2-3)

b. What characterized his background? (verses 4-5,9-11)
(Blaspheme means to speak evil or contemptuously of God or
sacred things.)

c. What reversed the direction of Paul's life? (verses 12-15)

d. How did Paul explain the gospel? (verse 23)

e. What did Paul ask Agrippa? Why is this question important?
(verse 27)

YOUR STORY

Now that you've seen how Paul told his story, work on a way to tell yours. Sharing how and why you chose to trust Christ can be one of the best ways to witness. It is particularly helpful in presenting Jesus Christ to relatives and close friends.

In telling your experience:

- *Make it personal—don't preach. Tell what Christ has done for you. Use "I," "me," and "my"—not "you."*
- *Make it short. Three or four minutes should be enough time to cover the essential facts.*
- *Keep Christ central. Always highlight what He has done for you.*
- *Use the Word of God. A verse or two of Scripture will add power to your story. Remember that the Word of God has a keen cutting edge.*

HOW TO PREPARE YOUR STORY

Try writing your story down on the next page just the way you would tell it to an unbeliever. Make the story clear enough that the person hearing it would know how to receive Christ.

Tell a little about your life before you trusted Jesus Christ, then about how you came to trust Him; and finally something of what it has meant to know Him — the blessing of sins forgiven, assurance of eternal life, and other ways your life or outlook has changed.

If you have been a believer for a number of years, be sure that your story includes some current information about the continuing effect of Christ in your life.

As you prepare your story, ask the Lord to give you opportunities to share it. Pray for two or three opportunities to witness in your neighborhood, at work, or at school.

MY STORY

BEFORE I trusted Christ:

HOW I trusted Christ:

SINCE I've trusted Christ:

19. List some people (family, friends, neighbors, coworkers, enemies) you know who don't know Jesus. What specifically can you do to introduce each of them to Jesus through your prayers, love, life, and words?

In conclusion, remember that you do not have the power in yourself to convince anyone of spiritual truth. The Holy Spirit convinces people of their need to know Christ (John 16:8). As you pray for those you want to share your story with, be sure to ask God to honor the proclamation of His Word, to convince people of their need, and to strengthen you as you share the gospel.

Name	Your Initiative

SUGGESTED VERSE FOR MEDITATION AND MEMORIZATION

1 Peter 3:15

But in your hearts revere Christ as Lord. Always be prepared to give an answer to everyone who asks you to give the reason for the hope that you have. But do this with gentleness and respect.

1 Peter 3:15

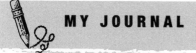

Read 2 Corinthians 2:14-17. Paul compares witnessing to the attraction of a sweet fragrance or aroma. What was particularly attractive or "fragrant" about the person (or people) who have influenced you to follow Christ? Journal about that awhile.

Then ask God to show you what is particularly attractive or "fragrant" about your life that might influence others to follow Christ. Also allow Him to reveal anything about you that may be turning others against Jesus. Journal about that, too. End by inviting Him to spread the sweet aroma of Christ through you.

► According to the principles of Scripture, we are to be witnesses of what we see, hear, and experience with Christ.

► We are witnesses by our actions of love, by our lifestyle, and by our speech, as we pray for others.

► The gospel advances in a variety of ways. A few are called to be mobile evangelists by crossing cultures with the gospel. Most of us are called to witness from our experience with Jesus as insiders to those we live and work among.

► Paul's spoken testimony provides a pattern for a witness: telling what our life was like before we met Christ, tell how we met Christ, and tell what our life is like since meeting Him.

Explore the fascinating story of Jesus sharing the gospel creatively with a Samaritan woman whom He met at the well (John 4:8-26). Observe what He did that touched her heart and won her trust in Him. Then consider what principles you can draw from this story to strengthen you as you tell your story.

An Encounter of Jesus from John 4:8-26

Verses	What Jesus Did	What You Can Do in Sharing the Good News
3-6	Took the initiative for social contact as He was going along	Intentionally hang out with people who don't know Christ yet as you go about your normal life
7-8	Established common interest conversationally	Develop authentic friendships around common interests, hobbies, and connections
9-15	Probed for interest	Get to know them; ask good questions about their lives and feelings; be conversational
9-17	Graciously dealt with deep issues (sexual & religious)	Be willing to engage on deep issues, but do it with humility and grace—not judgment
16-19	Honored appropriate limits	Don't go too far or beyond where your relationship allows you to go
16-19	Had appropriate, gracious attitude	Don't condemn or convey that you have all the answers or a perfect life; identify with their pain where you can
20-26	Focused on her concerns, but also returned to her deep inner needs	Don't get sidetracked into arguments
26	Brought the conversation to a clear close	Encourage them to make a decision

THE ESSENTIAL BIBLE STUDY SERIES FOR TWENTY-FIRST-CENTURY FOLLOWERS OF CHRIST.

DFD 1
Your Life in Christ
1-60006-004-8

This concise, easy-to-follow Bible study reveals what it means to accept God's love for you, keep Christ at the center of your life, and live in the power of the Spirit.

DFD 3
Walking with Christ
1-60006-006-4

Learn five vital aspects to living as a strong and mature disciple of Christ through this easy-to-understand Bible study.

DFD 4
The Character of a Follower of Jesus
1-60006-007-2

This insightful, easy-to-grasp Bible study helps you understand and put into action the internal qualities and values that should drive your life as a disciple of Christ.

DFD 5
Foundations for Faith
1-60006-008-0

This compelling Bible study will help you get a disciple's perspective on God, His Word, the Holy Spirit, spiritual warfare, and Christ's return.

DFD 6
Growing in Discipleship
1-60006-009-9

This study will provide insight and encouragement to help you grow as a true disciple of Christ by learning to share the blessings you've received from God.

DFD 7
Our Hope in Christ
1-60006-010-2

In this study of 1 Thessalonians, discover how to undertake a comprehensive analysis of a book of the Bible and gain effective Bible study principles that will last a lifetime.

DFD Leader's Guide
1-60006-011-0

The leader's guide provides all the insight and information needed to share the essential truths of discipleship with others, whether one-on-one or in small groups.

To order copies, call NavPress at 1-800-366-7788 or log on to www.navpress.com.

NAVPRESS

Discipleship Inside Out®